The France Alphabet

For the Discerning Traveller

by David Lawday

Published by Clink Street Publishing 2021

Copyright © 2021

First edition.

The author asserts the moral right under the Copyright, Designs and Patents Act 1988 to be identified as the author of this work.

All rights reserved. No part of this publication may be reproduced, stored in a retrieval system or transmitted, in any form or by any means without the prior consent of the author, nor be otherwise circulated in any form of binding or cover other than that with which it is published and without a similar condition being imposed on the subsequent purchaser.

ISBN:
978-1-914498-39-8 - paperback
978-1-914498-40-4 - ebook

Author's note to readers

The snap alphabetic look at France stands for characters, events and traditions that symbolize for me the French and their way of life. You may think some of my letter selections speak more for the past than the present, or indeed that some are misbegotten. Why F for Fashion, for instance, rather than for La Fontaine and his brilliant fables which continue to shape French morals from the cradle up? P is not for Paris -- though you would think it should be – only because the City of Light shimmers in any case right through the France alphabet. All I can say is that my letter selections were those that first came to me on the moment, which must mean something, and that they epitomize for me the France I have long lived in with my French wife. The cartoonish illustrations are also mine, there to give perhaps a supplementary intuitive glimpse into what makes the French the way they are. Finally, the whole was conceived in the time of the Covid pandemic. Will it have changed their ways? I doubt it.

A IS FOR ART

Art is…what exactly? A manner, you may say, of creating something with aesthetic appeal to the senses. France lives art. Take the French word for it. *Art de vivre*! The earthy side of the fine arts of painting, sculpture, music, architecture, literature. *Art de vivre* makes an art of everyday life. Cooking. Eating. Drinking. Dressing. Sauntering. Ogling. Protesting. Rebelling. Making love (a native boast?). Nowhere more than in France is quite such attention paid to attacking the daily round with creative flair.

France is the world home to art. To all art. The mighty Louvre in Paris houses the world's largest collection: half a million and more paintings, sculptures and sundry other masterpieces which naturally include the world's most famous painting, Leonardo da Vinci's *Mona Lisa*. The world itself originates between the bared thighs (*L'Origine du Monde*) of a languid Frenchwoman painted by a Frenchman. French Impressionists capture the world's fancy like no other school before or since. How extraordinary it is that the likes of Monet, Renoir, Degas, Manet, Cezanne, Morisot, Gauguin and the expatriate Dutchman Vincent van Gogh are all at their easels at much the same time. Foreign titans of the canvas from da Vinci himself to Picasso, as well as a passionate old dauber by the name of Winston Churchill, choose France to pose their palette – drawn by its colours, by the immense variety and beauty of its landscapes, by the artist's sense of simply being in the right place in the world to paint. The land of France itself is Mother Nature's own prize work of art.

Visitors, prepare to argue. No holds barred. The French are a ravenous and opinionated art public. Some irrepressible cultural sprite delights in making them quarrel over art. They will queue for hours to see an exhibition by some unknown artist so as to be able to argue over it. The French arts minister has political power high above that accorded to equivalent ministers (if they exist) in other countries. Art goes with power in France. No self-respecting president steps down without adorning the cityscape with some contentious architectural marvel for the nation to spar over – a great arch, a preposterously shaped art museum, a colossal new national library, an avant-garde concert hall. 'God help the statesman who meddles in art,' a chastened English prime minister of old once sighed. French leaders are not listening. Nor are the natives. Arguing over art, like cooking or rebelling, is part of *art de vivre*.

***

B IS FOR

BALZAC

Know Balzac and you know France. Honoré de Balzac (1799–1850) is the master chronicler of French society. He ribs it, dissects it, lays it bare in the 19th century yet might just as well have been doing so in this 21st – or at most any other time. Balzac's skill as a novelist is in exposing French mores eternal.

Corpulent, lank, unruly hair squeezed beneath a top hat, Balzac, son of a prominent provincial civil servant, strides forth on his mission armed with a lorgnette and a frightful cane topped with a gold knob encrusted with turquoise gems and strung with a young girl's gold necklace. With wry disdain for an ascendant bourgeoisie (try his novels *Père Goriot* and *Eugénie Grandet* for size), he devours life in Paris and the provinces in the 1830s–1840s, a time when modern France is taking shape. Through the all-seeing lorgnette he focuses on the fortunes and foibles of doctors and dandies, civil servants and tradesmen, bankers and whores, hostesses and charwomen, adulterers and usurers, officers and peasants, rich and poor – in sum the whole panoply of humankind issued from the French Revolution and the broken glories of Napoleon Bonaparte.

A similar thread – money – runs through each and every plot in Balzac's vast series of novels, ninety in all, bundled together in what he calls the *Comédie Humaine*. Envy of money. Sacrifices made for money. Lust for it. Lack of it. Owing of it. Squandering of it. Balzac is the very opposite of a miser himself, yet somehow knows all the feelings, all the torments, all the pleasures of a miser. Wifeless (though seldom short of a mistress) until close to his deathbed, he yet shows incomparable insight into women's innermost feelings. With Balzac, character is in the face: a shrew in her flat forehead, a banker in the manner of raising the eyebrows. a criminal in crossed front teeth.

Money is a vulture hovering over Balzac himself. The luxuries and opera nights he loves but cannot afford from his author's income so saddle him with debt that he is obliged to keep changing addresses and use false names to escape his creditors. He is permanently bursting with ideas. He tries business – a printing works then politics – to free himself from money woes. None succeed. Nothing for it, then, but to persist with a prying pen. At the age of forty he is writing up to twenty hours a day, commencing at midnight with a pot of coffee for company, inspired by the stillness of the night. Novels spring as rabbits from a hat, each one almost embarrassingly intrusive. This is literary realism on the loose, a looting of French private life with characters like the ambitious young social climber Rastignac appearing from one novel to the next.

At fifty-one Balzac expires unsurprisingly from exhaustion. His reward is already acquired: the status of France's favourite novelist.

***

C IS FOR

CROISSANT

The croissant demands that it be made and eaten in France. Baked elsewhere it will never taste as good, look as good or be as good. It takes a French baker working at a French oven to produce the real thing.

The magic of the croissant starts somewhere in a hefty ball of dough, first lightly salted and sugared, then rolled flat with butter, kneaded once more into a ball, rolled flat again for cutting into small triangles, each to be rolled over base-to-tip, twirled into crescent shape, then baked in the small hours to a flaky inner consistency and crispy outer crust for consumption with coffee at breakfast. The work must be done by hand, a French hand. The mass-produced industrial croissant is for the rest of the world's breakfast.

While necessarily French in the making, the croissant is not quite so French in origin. The most appealing, and you may accept authentic, version of its origin derives from 17th century Vienna as Ottoman Turk invaders flying their crescent-moon emblem stand blocked before the Austrian capital's ramparts. At length they choose a night to take the Christian stronghold by tunnelling in beneath the walls in the dark. On that tenebrous night in 1683 the citizens are asleep, all except for bakers on their way to light their ovens. Hearing a mysterious thud and clatter beneath their feet, the pastrymen alert the city's defenders who beat back the Ottoman assault. Whereupon, to fete their glorious role in saving the Christian capital, Viennese bakers treat the population to pastries cut in the shape of the Turks' retreating emblem.

Enter, close to a century on, the Austrian emperor's daughter Marie-Antoinette. Poor Marie-Antoinette, who is destined to lose her head for confusing cake with bread in the French Revolution, arrives in Paris from Vienna in 1770 to wed the French monarch Louis XVI. Smitten by pangs of longing for her home pastries, the queen soon orders a batch of the crescent-shaped treats sent in from Vienna. Fawning French courtiers who rush to try

C IS FOR CROISSANT

them create a sudden over-demand which Paris bakers meet by producing their own uniquely flaky version. By the time Marie-Antoinette goes to the guillotine the sans-culottes are developing an undying taste for it too.

Do not underrate the French baker. Throughout the land, from city to village, bakers are the captains of everyday street commerce. From first light their wares give off a unique odour. Walk by and you will have in your head the smell of France itself.

***

D IS FOR

DESCARTES

Beware of jousting with the French in intellectual argument. Should you try, blame Réné Descartes (1595–1650) for your predicament.

Descartes, born into the Loire Valley's landed gentry, has impregnated his compatriots through the ages with the gene of orderly thought. Give the educated French an issue to contest, however complex, and they will at once pare it down to three salient, irrefutable points ('firstly', 'secondly', 'lastly') to floor the gamest of opponents.

Descartes is a demon for methodical thinking. The rules he devises cover intuition, deduction, even doubt. Thus if, say, you are in doubt over some matter, your doubt proves that you are thinking, and to think is proof that you exist. *Cogito ergo sum*, as Descartes incontrovertibly has it. He reduces reasoning to near-mathematical method set out in his celebrated *Discours de la Méthode* (1637). To him philosophy is a tree whose roots are its metaphysical part, the trunk its physical part and the branches the signposts to all other territories of knowledge.

His method is a dangerous break with the splendid philosophical gyrations of Plato, Aristotle and the ancients. It antagonises, besides, the powerful Catholic Church whose myths are disinclined to sit the test of reason. Wounded clerics are hardly placated when Descartes claims, as if in atonement, that he is able to prove God exists. He is obliged to take his thinking cap abroad, where to ensure privacy he disguises his abode, giving his address in letters home as Utrecht for instance when he is in fact settled in Stockholm. The subterfuge is not unrelated to difficulties he encounters in rounding out his rules to cover morals. In the end he takes a pass on human morals, explaining with an ironic poke at France's absolute monarch of his day: 'First, there is no subject whereon malicious people find easier grounds to malign one, and second, I believe it is the task of kings alone or their ministers to meddle in setting morals for others.'

D is for DESCARTES

Great thoughtsmiths who come after Descartes salute his influence while contesting much of his logic. The Catholic Church never forgives him. You may ascribe his death in Stockholm at the age of fifty-three to a dose of arsenic fed him by a priest hellbent on protecting Church myth. His method is not so easily disposed of. Those orderly thought processes by which the French will batter you in argument carry a global brand name: Cartesian.

***

E IS FOR

EQUALITY

The France Alphabet

Liberté, Egalité, Fraternité. The patriotic trio holler inspiration at the French from the facades of their town halls, schools and public buildings. The middle bit of the national motto is a goal the French truly aspire to, trusting to God it will never materialise.

Social equality has biblical standing in French constitutional lore. It has held a revered place there since 1789 as a fervid Robespierre at first squares it off to cry *Liberté, Egalité, Fraternité ou la Mort* and only relinquishes his dread little suffix as brothers in revolt conclude that it carries rather too great a menace for their own necks. Equality in any case proves quite enough on its own to bring down the French throne. Louis XVI, the descendant of a thousand-year-old monarchy founded by Hugh Capet, is hauled to the guillotine as 'Citizen Capet'.

You may catch the French marching, waving banners and at times throwing rocks for social equality (for gender and LGBTQ equality too). There remains etched in the French mind the coaching in egalitarianism by the leading intellectuals of the post-1945 age, many of them so bewitched by Soviet communist ideals that they insist on imposing them on their compatriots even as Russians themselves itch to abandon them. The coaching has its legacy. The French are still inclined to tinker, Soviet-mindedly, with five-year economic plans. They are used to paying higher taxes than most other peoples, largely to finance a high level of welfare to promote – you have guessed it – social equality.

Only something, somehow, gets in the way.

In France inequality of wealth abounds. The figures look consistent. The richest 1% of the population possess 15% of the citizenry's wealth, and the richest 5% possess fully a third. This leaves half the nation, including indigent immigrants from North and Black Africa at the bottom end, sharing 8%. The generous social welfare system helps even things out to an extent. The equality gap would appear still more flagrant if the rich French were to crow about high income, which they do not. Or if heirs to 'old money' largesse were inclined to exhibit their fortunes, which they are not, content instead to register their worth by clinging to bygone titles (Duke, Duchess, Count, Countess) long since voided under the French republic, or if nothing else by eternalising the noble little particle 'de' fronting the family name.

In the end human nature is the national motto's undoing. The French are of course all equal under the law of the land. But *Liberté* and *Egalité* make impossible partners. 'Equality may be a right, but no power on earth can make it a fact.' Thus Balzac, who knows his compatriots better than most. So, yes, the French seek social equality – but only with those above them.

***

F IS FOR

FASHION

Paris. The Parisienne. Dior. Chanel. Saint Laurent. Cardin. Givenchy. Balmain. Gods of high fashion, like philosophers, artists and footballers, dispense with first names.

There is a secret to France's pre-eminence in fashion: its gods bank on the elegant and the seductive in the endless quest for originality, leaving the outright outrageous for others to fight over. Paris Fashion Week, a boom-boom, klieg-lit, techno-fest held twice a year, winter and summer, featuring scrawny girls parading swivel-kneed down elevated runways on behalf of rival designers, is the starting line in the fashion world's perennial race for newness – the chance for billionaire voyeurs and oil sheiks' wives in front row seats to purchase the prototype creation on show even as, backstage, its ready-to-wear version is going on offer and piratical scribblers are sketching the original to produce knock-down fast-fashion versions for the world's shopping malls. The destiny of this creation is foretold from the start. On first appearance, exciting. After a month chic. After six months fetching. After a year dowdy. In two years silly. In ten years quaint, in fifteen years charming, in twenty right back in style, all the rage.

French leadership in the fashion world begins beyond the mannequin's runway – on the boulevard. The passing Parisienne, no matter her age, has something special about her you may find hard to pin down. A small touch, simple, elegant, the throw of the scarf, the angle of the cap, a haughty look spiced with impishness, a gait that says she owns the city. Being a Parisienne is a state of mind, handed down mother to daughter no matter the social class, never overtly come-hither yet the more seductive for that, a look carefully studied in the bedroom mirror down to the last play of buttons, the last wisp of hair, so as to appear absolutely unstudied.

Fashion is in the French blood, a snappy gene implanted betimes by Sun King Louis XIV, who when not at war is a most elegant dresser, prettily shod, and demanding no less of his courtiers. The Sun King's court style is the admiration of the world, the making of a French brand that in time launches the great Paris fashion houses issuing from the *belle époque*.

Fashion is to France what high-tech is to America, the motor car to Germany, the royal family to Britain. Observe world markets and you will see that commerce at the highest end of *art de vivre* is dominated by three giant enterprises: the perfumer and beautician L'Oréal, the luxury conglomerate LVMH (Louis Vuitton Moët Hennessy) and the curiously named fashion and luxury goods group Kering, the last two of which between them own all top Paris fashion houses. Naturally all three are French. And Paris is forever Paris.

***

G IS FOR

DE GAULLE

A certain idea of France. With the obligingly Gallic name, the army general's pips and an imperious way with the French tongue, Charles de Gaulle (1890–1970) is well equipped to have a special feel for France's identity. His 'certain idea' of France is shaped by a past reaching back to the Roman conquest of Gaul which gives the country a special quality, an indestructible national grandeur.

Charles de Gaulle belies popular images of the typical Frenchman. He is unusually tall, oddly pear-shaped, canon-nosed, austere, more than a shade pompous, egotistical, cussed, a droll showman at times, a faithful spouse, sincere and without side. Yet he stands beside Vercingetorix, Joan of Arc, Louis XIV, Napoleon Bonaparte and comic-strip Asterix as France incarnate.

Anniversaries fall nicely rounded to celebrate Charles de Gaulle in worshipful triplicate. Take the year 2020. It marked the 130th anniversary of his birth into an upper-class Catholic family in industrial Lille, the son of a distinguished history professor; the 50th anniversary of his death; and the 80th anniversary of a crackling broadcast to Nazi-occupied France from London on 18 June 1940 that forever secures his legend – an appeal to his defeated people to resist Hitler, to resist their usurper collaborationist government in Vichy and pursue the struggle undaunted with 'me, General de Gaulle, French soldier and chief.'

The broadcast requires some gall. He is virtually unknown to the French at the time. But cometh the hour. De Gaulle's hour is World War Two. A graduate of France's Saint Cyr military academy who fights the Germans in World War One and is taken prisoner, he then rises through officer ranks as an inter-war military strategist. Sickened by France's failure to stop Hitler's invasion in 1940, he escapes to London convinced he carries French destiny on his general's shoulders. Alone in London with a few loyal French supporters he *is* France – the France he believes history has made her – and on the liberation of Paris in 1944, after constant spats with President Roosevelt and his London host

Winston Churchill, both of whom are irritated by his prickly arrogance, he strides down the Champs-Elysees in triumph, a deus ex radio-booth come to restore national pride after France's worst ever humiliation.

Beware of criticising Charles de Gaulle. There are those who do. But his pedestal is not for shaking. Countless miles of French streets bear his name, including the great roundabout at the Arc de Triomphe in Paris. As post-war president he rules benignly aloof, disdainful of political parties and indeed of parliament. A new French constitution is written to suit him and his 'certain idea'. He rides immense popular esteem through the country's economic resurrection of the 1950s and 1960s, surfing assassination attempts over his violently opposed decision to grant independence to Algeria, but comes up short in face of France's 1968 student uprising, an event which sees him scuttling off in secret, flummoxed for once, to the safety of a French army base in Germany. The brief disappearance is so uncharacteristic of the great man that most of the French either won't believe it or refuse to let it besmirch his image as national saviour. Two years later, aged eighty, he expires at his country retreat of Colombey in the somnolent vales of eastern France, henceforth a national shrine.

The general's prescient spirit resists the grave. Throughout his time as French president he personally bars Britain from joining the united Europe he champions. In his view the British are somehow not right for it. With hindsight, give him his due. The British, having gained membership of the European Union once he is gone, proceed over the years to confirm his opinion, then stumble blindly of out of it quite of their own accord with a rare sense of timing – no fault of the tall man this time – on the 50th anniversary of his death.

***

H IS FOR HUGO

The France Alphabet

Victor Hugo (1802–1885), god of French letters, is conceived, by his own account, in the heavens. That is, on a misty Vosges mountain peak where his soldiering father, prior to his promotion to general, ventures on leave from Napoleon Bonaparte's service to sport with his barely consenting Breton wife, who will soon leave him. The altitude is one from which the resulting Hugo junior is disinclined to descend.

Who is France's national writer? Is it Victor Hugo or his contemporary Henri Beyle? You may be faced with this conundrum should you happen among the French literati. Accept, first, that Balzac, while France's favourite author, is not in contention here due to laxity of style, nor, for this reason or that, are Molière, Racine, La Fontaine, Maupassant or Flaubert. Choose Beyle, alias Stendhal, and you will win stylists' applause. His deliciously malicious *Le Rouge et Le Noir* must stand as the best French novel of all time. But in the broader French mind there is really no contest. Hugo, immense Hugo, colossal Hugo, the bard who casts a warty hunchback into the world's nightmares and whose state funeral brings out the entire population of Paris in homage, indeed inhabits the heavens. More French streets are named for him than for General de Gaulle.

Hugo intends to change the world. As it happens, however, the world of his early days is changing too fast for his prodigious pen to shape. Rather he changes with the changes – the triumphs and precipitous fall of Napoleon, the restoration of bewigged Bourbon kings in Napoleon's place, the restored crown's fusty collapse into a liberal monarchy, popular revolts galore, and finally a coup by Bonaparte's nephew to install himself as Emperor. Hugo rides the currents from arch-monarchist to revolutionary socialist, from romantic to riot-monger, from self-exile to home-rushing patriot. Out of it all, in foaming spate, come plays, passionate verse and novels that spread his fame across the world with *Notre Dame de Paris* and *Les Misérables*.

Hugo is verbose. Hugo is overbearing. He appears fickle, especially to the many mistresses called upon to satisfy his voracious desires. He is vain. Impulsive. A notorious tightwad. But through it all he holds firmly to patriotic principles, among them unbending repudiation of Emperor Napoleon III's coup against an infant French republic which Hugo's own pen has fought to establish. Rather than bow to the man he dubs 'Napoleon the Little', Hugo sentences himself to endless exile from his beloved Paris in England's drear Channel Islands. He stays away for nineteen years, returning in whitebeard triumph to Paris the minute Napoleon III falls, his prestige lofted to the skies by monumental works loosed on the French public from exile.

On Hugo's death at the august age of eighty-three, worshipping multitudes numbering some two million at his funeral form the largest crowd ever to have gathered in Paris, then the largest city in the world – an event confirming his rank. Victor Hugo, France's national writer.

***

I IS FOR INTELLECTUAL

The France Alphabet

French intellectuals announce themselves. As a doctor professes to be a doctor or a plumber a plumber, a French intellectual will state matter-of-factly in public: 'Speaking as an intellectual...' 'An intellectual like myself...' 'As an intellectual, I will say...' Only in France does the intelligentsia talk so. You may wonder whether its members are aware how self-important it sounds.

France breeds intellectuals. At age 16–17, lycée students sitting their *baccalauréat* examination are obliged to write essays on questions such as: Is it possible to escape from time? What use is it to explain a work of art? Can one renounce truth? This constitutes the philosophy part of the school *bac*. The breeding works. There is much call on professional thoughtsmiths in the social media age to share their wisdom, especially if it comes supported by an *ism* they represent. Present-day French novelists brandish the breeding. Please, no intrigue! No plot! The intellectual's literary instinct is introspective – a trawl through the nooks and crannies of the mind. A tome of 350 pages that rambles over a thousand mental pickings will be published not as a novel but as an essay. Hail to the *bac*.

The mind of the French intellectual can of course fill a great book. With Montaigne, Montesquieu and Voltaire it ignites and fans the Enlightenment. Much later it drives intellectual warfare into the left-versus-right political pit, turning outright insurrectional betimes, impelled, as Jean-Paul Sartre disingenuously defines it, 'to meddle in things that don't concern me.' It can, besides, show mighty courage. The brave Claude Levi-Strauss, when not tiresomely engaged in fielding misdirected requests for shipments of blue jeans, sets himself the task of finding a mathematical formula to define myth, eventually reducing everything from Valhalla and Camelot to Romulus, Remus and the Virgin Birth to the pellucid equation:

$Fx(a): Fy(b) = Fx(b): Fa-1(y)$

F for fable? The smaller multipliers go to the grave with philosopher-anthropologist Levi-Strauss, a model of the breeding.

***

J IS FOR JOAN OF ARC

You are entitled to feel sad for Joan of Arc (1412–1431), who meets a horrifying end and serves, besides, as an icon for France's latterday extreme nationalists. She is moreover obliged to compete for the nation's affections with Marianne, a mythical priestess who symbolises the living French republic much as Joan herself stands for an archaic order of Catholic valour and monarchy absolute.

Joan of Arc is no myth. She is real. And, in her day, odd. An illiterate peasant girl from Lorraine who, while reliably examined to be female and a virgin, dresses as a male, wears a man's short-back-and-sides, dons heavy medieval armour and is driven by 'voices'. At the tender age of seventeen, with no military training, she rides into battle to save king and country with the Christian fervour of a knight crusader, making herself a world legend.

The voices of God and the saints that speak to adolescent Joan in the remote Lorraine village of Arc, near Domrémy, direct her to the city of Orleans, whither a despondent French claimant to the French throne is somehow talked into sponsoring her unlikely mission to save the city and his dynasty. Her mission is to deliver Orleans from a siege by English troops in the turbulent year of 1429, a time when England, likewise pressing its claim to the French throne, already occupies close to half of France and is bent on adding the important city to its crown possessions.

Orleans you say!

J IS FOR JOAN OF ARC

Joan's exploits in Orleans doubtless fall short of her cleaving through the English soldiery with flashing maiden's sword. But her arrival in knight's shining armour does seem to inspire the defenders, who manage to drive off the English. The triumph enables her besides to fulfil a second half of the mission the voices have set her: to escort a grateful French dauphin to Rheims to be crowned king as Charles VII.

France and the monarchy are saved, Christian faith rewarded.

Honoured far and wide as the Maid of Orleans, Joan is alas captured soon after by a feudal French rival of Charles VII, the Duke of Burgundy, who sells her to the English to dispose of. Her trial in English-occupied Rouen before a quisling French bishop as her judge turns mainly on the voices and her male garb, which bespeak witchery to the court. At nineteen, convicted of heresy, she is burned at the stake in the Rouen marketplace.

In the years and centuries that follow Joan runs into heavyweight critics. The Sun King Louis XIV expunges her from history, refusing to believe his radiant dynasty can owe its survival to a peasant wench. Voltaire ridicules her on behalf of the Enlightenment. And soon bare-bosomed Marianne makes her mythical appearance with the French Revolution, an utterly feminine symbol of a new republic representing just about the opposite of all that Joan stands for when eventually canonised.

There is great romance in Saint Joan for all the censure, armour plate and crossdressing – the romance of the spirit of a girl so young, battling all odds and paying for her patriotic endeavours on a crackling pyre that burns the life out of her. The romance it is that earns her a far more glorious place in the French mind than that pressed upon her by extreme nationalists. Joan of Arc: national heroine.

***

K IS FOR

KISS

French kiss. The French do a lot of kissing. On each cheek for hello as well as goodbye. The courteous male's brush of the lips to the back of a woman's hand. Small children, dutifully, on meeting grownups. Teenagers, rat-a-tat rounds on each cheek in a ritual of group belonging. Politicians in greeting, out of gratitude or bored duty. Businessfolk, in treacherous boardrooms. The kiss of life, as merited. Kiss of death, as warranted. And in lovemaking, the languorous tongue-to-tongue variety (verb active; to *french*).

In truth France owns no universal patent on palate-laving rapture. The ancient Romans delighted in the lingual quishabout. You may be sure it persisted through the Dark Ages and the Enlightenment, however prone to ups and downs in universal favour depending on how far plagues and epidemics shift social mores from lax to puritanical and back again. Hygiene? Never mind hygiene. Clinical studies calculate that it sends 250 different bacteria and 40,000 parasites slithering about entranced partners' mouths. The point is this: compared with even the dreamiest clench-lipped embrace, it increases exponentially the prospects for going all the way. It leads inexorably into bed – with the glad bonus of strengthening the network of facial muscles that prevent wrinkles.

The 'french' tag derives from the First World War, when primmer kissing habits of allied soldiers sent to France are loosened by close encounters with native womenfolk. For British and American troops raised on late-Victorian custom the experience is unforgettable, one to stow at the top of the kitbag for the return home.

The French themselves seem hardly aware they have lent their name to the salivary step towards bed. When they care to put a name to it, they have one of their own: a *galoche*, as in galosh, welly, wader.

***

L IS FOR

LOUIS XIV

French grandeur streams in dazzling rays from Louis XIV, the Sun King. Under Louis (1638–1715) France becomes the most powerful realm in Europe. Unified, secure, prosperous, frontiers expanded. The French court glitters, the model for manners, style and taste. As royal residence Louis transforms a shabby hunting lodge at Versailles into a palace of unrivalled magnificence, a wonder of the world. Towards the end of his reign, the longest in European history, his sun will sink. But ask the French who gives them most to be proud of and there is one answer. It is not Napoleon. Louis XIV is the *Grand Roi*.

How is it all done?

Louis is born fortunate. The French world presents him with unforeseen opportunities from the start and he makes the most of them. He is five years old when he becomes king, but by the time he assumes personal power from unusually supportive regents (his widowed mother Anne of Austria and the astute Italian chief minister Cardinal Mazarin) an age of chaos has turned into one of unlikely promise for the French throne. Civil war and provincial uprisings at home have obligingly petered out. Equally obligingly, France's foreign rivals appear paralysed: England in post-republican daze on Oliver Cromwell's death; Spain vanquished; Germany split into countless statelets; Austria mollified by Queen Anne's motherly hold on her French son. What better time for France at last to gain her 'natural' shape?

L IS FOR LOUIS XIV

His authority absolute, Louis turns to the task with a will. France is far from having today's shape in the mid-17th century. Having strengthened his army, Louis wages war beyond his frontiers to incorporate Flanders in the north, great swathes in the east reaching to the Rhine (indeed well across it into the German Rhineland) and in the Alps. Each territorial gain becomes part of France, through the efforts of his army engineer-in-chief, the tireless Vauban, who consolidates the expansion with magnificent fortifications built around France's entire perimeter, land and shore. At home his crafty finance minister Colbert uses the years of rare domestic tranquillity to fill the royal coffers. Since the realm is for once united, with sovereign lords from the provinces at last bowing to Louis' monarchy absolute, from now on everything will be decided from Paris. Now is born the highly centralised state that France forever favours. Peace at home also permits Louis to complete the lavish work on Versailles and to sport there with his many mistresses, scarcely hiding them from his Spanish wife Maria Theresa, who nonetheless bears him six children.

In time Louis creates problems for himself – first by expelling French Protestants to no advantage, nor for any good reason, then by underestimating the manner in which the rest of Europe, egged on by England's William of Orange, is at length getting together to halt French assertiveness. On his death after a seventy-two-year reign, popular unrest in France is astir, in particular over taxation. Louis frets over what is to follow. But it isn't the Sun King who sighs 'Après moi le deluge'. The lament will come from his grandson Louis XV, who also misreads the storm runes, for the deluge holds off until long after both are gone – threescore years and more in the Sun King's case – as Paris street mobs storm the Bastille.

***

M IS FOR METRO

The France Alphabet

Apologies to Molière, masterful 17th century tease of the French bourgeoisie, who more than merits the place here for his malicious comedies that forever enthral French theatregoers. But the Paris Metro won't be shunted aside. It is part of *art de vivre*.

Metro underground trains come every two minutes. Its stations are situated close enough to each other so that you can still walk to where you want to go should you have been deep in a book or conversation and missed your stop by one, or two. Nowhere in Paris are you more than a few minutes' walk from the nearest Metro station. Its platforms will generally lie a single flight of stairs below street level. *Voltaire. Maison Blanche. Colonel Fabien.* Station names are a ride through abstruse corners of Paris life, clues to a monument, an insurrection, a bordello, a poet, a doctor, any manner of statesman (though not Robespierre or Philippe Pétain, both Metro outcasts). The carriages are neither so comfortable as to induce down-and-outs to retain their seat day and night, nor so uncushioned as to make you want to move aboveground for a traffic-jammed bus. The network is automated, trains mostly riding on rubber tyres, their onrush a whisper, barely enough to announce their imminent coming. They arrive in a light breeze.

That is the Metro on a good day.

With its *art deco* wrought-iron station entrances, some still announcing **METROPOLITAIN** beneath their original fanned-glass *belle époque* awnings, the Metro is as much a symbol of Paris as the

Eiffel Tower. As high winds may close the tower, things may conspire to go wrong in the Metro. Mysterious pauses are not infrequent. The loudspeaker-announced 'technical problem' that halts your journey may involve some driver not turning up for a change of shift. The 'incident' at a single station (an altercation perhaps involving a ticket inspector, or someone fainting on the platform) will close the entire line. Furthermore the personnel of the Metro, a public enterprise, seldom hesitate to walk out for one reason or another.

But relax. Consider the safety record. The Metro's last and only catastrophic accident occurred in 1903 – three years after the first line opens. Then it is that fire in a prototype wooden carriage causes a tunnel stampede in which eighty-four passengers are crushed to death or asphyxiated.

METROPOLITAIN lines make a pretty map. The criss-cross underground mosaic is at first confined within the Paris city perimeter traced by towering 19th century walls long since demolished. After the 1914–18 war the network fingers out to close suburbs, and from the 1970s onwards a Johnny-come-lately underground cousin extending to far suburbs, a bleak speedster called the RER (Reseau Express Regional), burrows in beneath it, inter-connecting with the Metro in city depths at busy points like the Arc de Triomphe and Les Halles. But RER stations are far apart and the charmless caverns of its platforms are long enough to host a marathon. A still deeper, faster, bleaker, automated cross-Paris underground line making scarcely a stop is under construction to whoosh into the future.

Know, visitors, that the underground racers are for suburbanites, who outnumber city-dwelling Parisians more than four to one and don't much care where they happen to be when riding beneath the avenues of the city. Genuine Parisians stick with the venerable Metro. It has soul. With the Metro you always know just where you are.

***

N IS FOR

NAPOLEON

Napoleon Bonaparte (1769–1821) is an enigma. Matchless source of French national pride for some. Deep stain upon it for others. But those French who sit on the moral fence over Napoleon will usually tumble, if tumble they must, on the side of pride. How not to feel some inner glow at carrying the greatest conqueror since Julius Caesar in your genes.

Napoleon's ambitions amaze in his time, and amaze now. He pulls France out of the coma of a staggering revolution while the embers of 1789 still burn. He aspires to conquering all continental Europe with his invincible Grande Armée, and does so. He is bolder than brass. He stands on a cliff on France's Channel coast, fixes his spyglass on the white cliffs of Dover and orders a tunnel built beneath the waves for the conquest of England, an ambition he would quite possibly have achieved had not yet more pressing martial concerns called him elsewhere. And all the while – having shot to power via precocious exploits as a revolutionary army gunnery captain and lightning-fast military promotion, whence his self-promotion to French emperor – he is devising a new social code for France, modernising its infrastructure, planning splendid monuments, creating a continental trading

system to hobble rival England and jousting with the Catholic Church (he imprisons the poor pope).

Napoleon is good for the tottering France he rises out of the rustic Corsican gentry to rule. The French look to the triumphal young warrior for release from revolution, civil war and the absolute power of kings. Shaking off his modest beginnings and a twanging Italian accent never comes as easily, however, as winning battles. Even when placing his brothers and sisters on the thrones of Europe, he himself struggles in vain to acquire the courtly Parisian manners he admires. Napoleon is a snob, a trait that accompanies his slide from national saviour to despot. The good he has done France he blindly undoes. Invasions of Spain and ultimately of Russia, neither of which serve much purpose beyond his ego, are his empire's death knell. Close counsellors like Prince Talleyrand, his diplomatic brain, believe he has gone mad and so contrive for the good of France to stop him. Napoleon rides France from the heights of exaltation to the depths of defeat and humiliation.

Those who cherish him prefer to rest on the heights he scaled (a Bonapartist political movement continues to rally in France). Those who regard him with distaste and unease remember the hundreds of thousands of Frenchmen of the Grande Armée who die satisfying his lust for conquest, the harsh conscription methods he introduces, and the France he leaves behind – a country so stricken and demoralised that it is forced to restore the royalty of the rheumy *ancien régime*.

Take your pick. Grandeur or grief. But remember this. French devotees and sour critics of Napoleon alike get no little satisfaction from knowing that one of their own fascinates the world like very few others in human history.

***

O IS FOR OCCUPATION

The France Alphabet

Hitler's occupation of France (1940–44) has left an indelible scar on the French psyche. The wound, however old, is forever raw. Several bygone invaders, England's Henry V among them, have taken Paris. None has implanted in the French soul quite the shame and distress of the Nazi occupation. The image of German jackboots tramping down the Champs-Elysees through Napoleon's Arc de Triomphe remains the stuff of French nightmare.

The occupation is so dark a time for France that the nation's postwar conscience long declines to struggle with it, in particular the level of collaboration it has caused. Better embrace a myth: France in defeat has done its level best to resist. Only when the urge comes to examine the truth, twenty years and more after the unpalatable event, do the French start to see themselves more clearly. Indeed fifty years pass before a French president (Jacques Chirac) accepts that it is indeed France, eternal France – not merely an impostor France run by wretched impersonators gathered in the spa resort of Vichy – which bears responsibility in the hour of military defeat for installing a government to collaborate with Hitler, to impose Nazi laws on the French nation and round up Jews for dispatch to Nazi death camps.

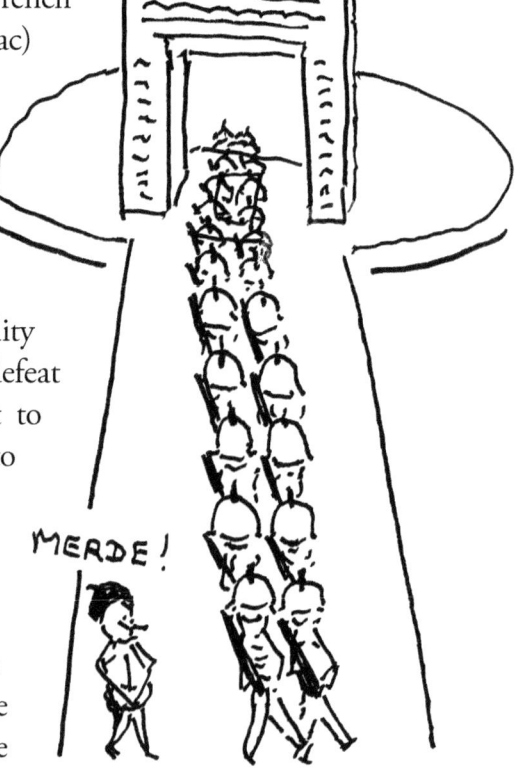

From the moment the allied invasion of France permits General de Gaulle to leave London and re-enter Paris, his priority is to bandage the wound. *Paris outraged! Paris broken! Paris martyred! But Paris liberated!* De Gaulle knows the real story. There has been no popular uprising against the occupation. But his task at the Liberation is to restore order and keep power out of the hands of the Communists, who have led a tiny domestic minority (mostly spirited, often Jewish youths) in active physical resistance to the Nazis. The comforting tidings he brings Paris are that the French have liberated themselves. Rejoice. Be proud. Popular resistance to Nazi tyranny has prevailed.

Thus buoyed, the majority of the French who have lived with Vichy, enthusiastically or not, are able to come out and attest to how they have all along been *résistants* at heart. The purge that follows – the execution or public degradation of flagrant *collabos*, of Vichy officials, of informers, of those who have engaged in atrocities against fellow citizens, those who have enriched themselves from the occupation, women who have openly frolicked with the enemy – is short-lived. Of more than 7000 French citizens sentenced to death, just one in five is executed.

There is a way to soothe the French over their wound. They may justifiably ask: What would you have done in our place? How would you have resisted such an invader? There is of course no knowing. Survival is a human priority. In the uneasy search for a response, best shake the head.

***

P IS FOR PROUST

Every country needs its great unreadable author. Marcel Proust (1871–1922) is to France what James Joyce is to Ireland and, in the case of stamina-challenged readers, what Thomas Mann is to Germany and Henry James to America (the latter confesses he can't abide to read his own best-known work).

One measure of the unreadable author is to be singled out as the greatest there ever was by less renowned writers who hope thereby to promote their own wares. A more calculatable measure is that of most readers, who, be they ever so willing, cannot get beyond the first sixty pages before drowsiness, or indeed coma, defeats them. Shamed by defeat, you try again a year later and the same thing happens. And the year after that. Sixty pages. Maybe fifty. Upon that fifty milestone Marcel Proust stakes his place in the international pantheon of literary greatests.

Proust-slumber is a pleasurable daze brought about by wave upon mellifluous wave of soul-searching reminiscence washing over one in an ocean swell of commas and subordinate clauses. Proust, an asthmatic frail of health from childhood, possesses the literary lungs of a marathon runner. His parentheses float up into the air like little balloons that stay aloft until they eventually descend, semi-forgotten, to find an apt landing place.

Proust's novels on love and jealousy, pride and hurt, high life and vulgarity in the fashionable world of *belle époque* Paris melt, virtually without plot, into the seven volumes of his massive work *À La Recherche du Temps Perdu*. The intrigue lies in what goes on in the minds of mundane Parisians like Charles Swann and the elusive Odette in the opening volume. Nothing physical. Nothing violent, except in the tortured heart. The background music is in the description of Paris salon furnishings, the drawn curtain of a fiacre.

Proust himself, a slender figure with deep dark eyes and raven moustache, leads the life of upper-class Parisian lounger, a young artist about town 'swanning' between literary soiree here and musical soiree there. These are the scenes from which he draws the characters for his novels. A duel he fights with pistols over a critic's nasty book review is so languid an affair that neither he nor his critic emerges remotely scathed. He makes no play of his homosexuality but scarcely hides it either in his writings. His privileged existence, the worth of which he contemplates with silken irony, is the gift of wealthy parents: his Catholic father a distinguished professor of medicine, his highly cultured Jewish mother a doting companion in life (his holidays outside Paris are invariably spent with her alone). After her death he turns literary recluse, spending his last fifteen years on his massive oeuvre before dying of pneumonia, aged fifty-one.

Proust's place in the pantheon of unreadable greatests? Know that a single page of a hand-annotated Proust manuscript can sell under the auctioneer's hammer for the price of an opulent Paris mansion. A single page. A most readable length.

***

Q IS FOR QUEBEC

Quebec really ought no longer weigh on French hearts. But it does. Few things would tickle French fancy more than to see the vast Canadian province, France's very first colony, becoming an independent nation. It would feel somehow akin to Quebec coming home. Observe such sentiment in the fond name the French use for it: *La Belle Province*. This is an affair of the heart.

Don't put Quebec independence beyond the realm of the French imagination. It is not so long since General de Gaulle, with a last patriotic fling as French president, went to the heart of the new world's northern bounds – the great swathe that French kings initially named *Nouvelle France* – and stirred a diplomatic hornet's nest by openly encouraging it to pull free from Canada. *Vive le Quebec libre*, he roars from the city hall balcony in Montreal, the province's largest city. While no doubt transported on the moment by nostalgic passion, de Gaulle isn't also averse to giving the finger to the neighbouring Americans and indeed to the British, who had long since forced France to cede the land it colonised in the 17th century.

FICHTRE!

Q IS FOR QUEBEC

Eight million Quebecers, inhabitants of a vast domain of prairies and subarctic forest three times the size of France, may feel a little less close to their original colonisers than the French like to think. Hemmed in on all sides by Canada's 'English' provinces and the United States, Quebecers know where their practical interests lie. Twice in recent times they have voted down the chance to take independence. But their Frenchness won't die. The province's sole official language remains resolutely French, spoken with fur-trader twang and laced with a quaint vernacular used by 17th century French explorers. Venturing from the Atlantic far into the Gulf of Saint Lawrence, the explorers first plant France's royal standard – the emblem of territorial possession – at the point where the Saint Lawrence River narrows, which Algonquin Indians call Kebek.

The tenacity of Quebec's Frenchness endears itself to the metropolitan French for its will to survive against relentless pressure from North America's pervasive Englishspeak. The wonder is that it survives at all. It is a far hoarier survivor than colonial Frenchness elsewhere in the world. The flag is planted at Kebek a good two centuries before France throws herself into the European powers' hectic race to colonise in the last half of the 19th century. Since France wishes to convince herself that this is a moral mission to civilise hapless races across the planet, the experience is bittersweet. The civilising credo at length arouses ungrateful resentment among its beneficiaries. In Indo-China and North Africa France find herself ensnared in debilitating and humiliating colonial wars which only postpone the granting of independence to all her main charges before the 20th century is out.

Quebec is a happier story. There, after planting the flag, the mission is to bring in French immigrants from the motherland, settle them as peaceably as possible with the Algonquins and launch a nice trade in furs. So, no war (except a bit later with the rival British). That sweetens sentiment towards Quebec. Enough to keep the French dreaming.

***

R IS FOR
REVOLUTION

The French Revolution is *the* revolution. A uniquely staggering event. One that launches human society upon a new path for good and all. The bliss that 'twas in that dawn to be alive is none the less the joy felt by a romantic English poet looking on from afar. French sentiment on the volcano that erupted in the Paris of 1789 is rather more equivocal.

There never has been a revolution like the French one. The Russian one is an awed offspring. By comparison Oliver Cromwell's rampage against the throne in England that precedes it is merely a puritan warrior's tilt for power, in so far as once Charles I's head is removed and the Roundhead leader falls, things resume much as before. The same with the American Revolution. After the American colonies overthrow British rule, well, American society goes its way pretty much as before, slavery to the fore.

In France it is different. Out of the sacking of the Bastille there springs a social contract new to mankind, one stamped with as prettily named a freedom charter as ever there was – the Declaration of the Rights of Man. This is the Enlightenment coming to power, a mighty leap into the social unknown after a thousand years of rule by absolute monarchs backed by the feudal nobility and the Catholic Church. Removing Louis XVI's head is almost an afterthought. What matters is reshaping society, making everyone equal before the law, at liberty to think, act and choose their labour.

Royal courts in the rest of Europe, all atremble, are naturally galvanised into undoing the abominable occurrence. Assistance comes from within the revolution itself in the form of suicidal feuds breaking out between bourgeois reformers and radical ideologues. As royalist counter-revolutionary forces gather on France's borders, ideologues led by Robespierre set themselves a ruthless mission to save *their* revolution by sending moderate comrades-in-revolt to the guillotine, along with priests, aristocrats and royalist sympathisers. 'Bliss' descends into indiscriminate bloodletting. The Terror.

R IS FOR REVOLUTION

Travellers, beware of abusing the French Revolution, for all its horrors. The conservative-minded French will have you deplore it. Many more, though, will have you remember the miraculous way in which through thick and thin, through exaltation and terror, through all efforts by Europe's monarchs to crush it, the bold human spirit at its origin prevails and in time spreads across the world. A long-term enterprise.

***

S IS FOR SEX

The French are open about sex, which is unusual only in so far as most other peoples, while more than ready to indulge, are not.

The French are comfortable with sex in pretty well any form it might take. The bawdy Renaissance monk Rabelais launches an explicit tradition pursued by the Marquis de Sade, by anonymous chroniclers of innocent chambermaids' wide-eyed adventures, and by countless reputable authors and documentarists, none of whose works is meant for hiding in a back drawer. Openness is the rule, be it for bygone French kings flaunting their royal mistresses or silk-knickered can-can girls delivering show-it-all high kicks. It comes to cinema screens – for the first time for general public viewing – with a slender French sylph skipping all but naked over the hot sands of Saint Tropez. Ah! Brigitte Bardot. The Sex Kitten. Pioneer of cinema sex for all eyes.

A woman who has sex appeal is said in France to have *chien*. Dog! This is telling. *Chien* lies not in dress (or undress), nor necessarily in a pretty face or silhouette. It implies some indefinable natural drawing power, some animal quality. Sex has little or no link with morality for the French. It is kennel pleasure, as likely distinct from romantic love as a token of it. It cannot therefore be sinful. No position for having sex is wrong.. No taboos. No shamefulness. It is altogether possible for a couple to have wanton sex on a first date if the mood is right rather than quibble, No, wait! We may spoil a blissful relationship if we don't wait. Like Madame Bovary, the French like to think they are romantic, but they are not. Nor is fidelity in sex required, though it may be if a relationship *does* ensue, at which point sexual jealousy of a violent Latin order may come of it. A corpse may indeed be left on the floor. While the *crime de passion* is not encouraged, it is however punishable with unique leniency under French law, at times pardoned.

Openness about sex has produced the universally accepted cliché that the French are good at it. Incurably libidinous. Oh là là! Before setting foot in France most foreigners, Anglo-Saxons in particular, are convinced this is so. Saucy Paris Madames and their girls live on in the lace and velvet of foreign fantasy. This is tickled up by the unique popular indulgence the French show towards their leaders' sexual indiscretions. A president's infidelities – the rule rather than the exception – invariably earn more winks than lost support from French voters.

Remember too. Paris is a city that come Saint Valentine's Day flashes a message on its official electronic municipal information boards advising: 'The flower shops of Paris give 50% off on your second bouquet! Do not forget your mistress.'

T IS FOR

TALLEYRAND

The France Alphabet

You can do all you desire with bayonets, Sire, except sit on them

Prince Talleyrand, without writing a single play nor yet a sonnet, is France's answer to Shakespeare. The Shakespeare, that is, whose best lines dinner-table raconteurs delight in quoting. 'As Shakespeare had it…' In France Talleyrand (1754–1839) has the same distinction. 'As Talleyrand put it…' He is thus obliged, like the bard, to take credit for more badly mangled aphorisms than ever entered his head.

Charles-Maurice de Talleyrand-Perigord, prince, bishop (defrocked), statesman, ace of diplomats and much of rank besides, has a lot of choice lines to his name. Wisdom grows with irony in a career as diverse as his. Club-footed from birth, he graduates from bewigged and powdered salon star of the *ancien régime* to co-author of the French Revolution's earth-shaking Declaration on the Rights of Man, from hapless exile in America's raw early days of independence to diplomatic brain of the all-conquering Napoleon Bonaparte, and ultimately, upon deciding

T IS FOR TALLEYRAND

that Napoleon's departure is necessary for the good of France, from the warrior emperor's closest adviser to architect of his fall.

What makes Talleyrand a constant source of dinner-table wit is his unflustered quotability. *Never speak ill of yourself, your detractors will always do it better… Better leave to tomorrow what you can perfectly well do today… To be admired in society always listen closely to those telling you things you already know.* Having married a notoriously scatty beauty, he has counsel for gentlemen of repute: 'Always marry a woman known to be an idiot. She embarrasses only herself. An intelligent wife's foolishness embarrasses her husband.'

Talleyrand's split with Napoleon produces the epoch's most memorable dialogue. The harassed emperor, furious with his foreign policy chief for criticising his war-making in Spain behind his back, summons a meeting of imperial dignitaries and breaks into a tirade directed specifically at the phlegmatic Talleyrand in his high imperial vestments, threatening to have him hanged before spluttering: 'You are a…a…a shit in a silk stocking.' To which Talleyrand, unmoved, responds for all to hear as Napoleon stalks out, 'What a pity, such a great man and so ill-mannered.'

A pity, too, that Talleyrand is chiefly remembered for ineffable dictums. His way with words achieves more than the dubious right to be quoted. After helping to spare France from Napoleon's excesses, he proceeds by artful diplomacy to rescue it as a sovereign state. For there are those among Napoleon's European victors who aim thereafter to carve France up into a series of harmless separate statelets. When they meet at the Congress of Vienna (1815) to redraw the map of Europe and decide on France's fate, Talleyrand is there, alone, to defend his now defenceless country. Armed with cool, withering logic and, just as persuasively, with the best table in town (he brings his renowned Paris chef Carême to Vienna for the occasion), he puts the vengeful victors aright. Thank Talleyrand, then, for ensuring that France is France.

***

U IS FOR

URINAL

While open about sex, the French – in this instance mostly males – are also uniquely open about relieving themselves in public. Look aside if you will. It is difficult, though, to avoid seeing them at it by the roadside, against a wall or at the next hedge. This is a cultural matter, conduct long given official blessing in the form of the *urinoir*, a street structure as open as can be short of providing no cover at all.

The *urinoir* – or *vespasienne* by its fancier name – is a small, circular iron shed painted dark green and open to the elements save for an outer screen that hides communal users' torsos from public sight, leaving heads, shoulders and legs exposed. It simultaneously accommodates several needful males, each relieving himself into the flowing spout of a drain in the middle. True, the *urinoir* is a dwindling, indeed vanishing, presence on France's streets and squares, victim of prissy municipal decrees. But it holds an abiding place in French folklore.

What sharper caricature of French society than the social frictions caused by a newly erected urinal in fictional Clochemerle, a wine-growing village in Beaujolais. Clochemerle's Communist mayor and his liegeman, the socialist schoolmaster, plant the malodorous structure in the church square, ostensibly for the convenience of vineyard peasants but equally as one in the eye for the squire's lady, the curate, the notary and the forces of village reaction who indignantly oppose it. The 1930s novel so captures eternal strains in French society that Clochemerle is an enduring part of the French language. Its meaning: a preposterous squabble.

Open urinals first come to Paris in the 1830s in support of royal edicts forbidding citizens to relieve themselves against the nearest wall, as is the prevailing custom. The capital installs 500 and more under the genteel name of *vespasiennes* after Roman Emperor Vespasian, who taxes the Roman citizenry's urine upon its collection by tradesmen to treat wool for dying. The *vespasienne* soon gains a street partner in Paris – the cylindrical Morris column with its onion top, a colourful structure designed not for quick personal convenience but for promotional bill-sticking by theatres, shops and restaurants.

The Morris column, named after its creator, a Paris printer, outlives the *urinoir* as a boulevard symbol not only because it looks and smells better. A reputation the *urinoir* earns over the years as a then illicit haunt for queers hastens its decline. Among those once caught in a police raid at a well-frequented boulevard spot is France's Minister of Information who, when queried as to his presence, announces, 'I am informing myself naturally.'

***

V IS FOR

VOLTAIRE

Voltaire (1694 -1778) is the ultimate free-thinker, which requires some boldness for a Frenchman of his times when blasphemers are getting their tongues ripped out, non-believers face being tortured to death and those who as much as offend the crown are thrown into the dark dungeons of the Bastille. The human liberties that burst upon the world with the French Revolution to put an end to such routine horrors are, however, the fruit of his harrying pen.

Voltaire's ammunition for his assault on the intolerance of France's absolute monarchy and the Catholic Church is wicked irony. His novelistic masterpiece *Candide*, among the bestselling works in all French literature, tells of a quest for human happiness which pitches its innocent hero from one impossible horror to the next, each succeeding disaster a mirror to the arbitrary bullying of the monarchy and the Church – until he has to acknowledge there can be no happiness, not with things as they are. All anyone can do in the circumstances is to accept one's lot. *Il faut cultiver son jardin.*

Voltaire's first career steps appear inconsistent with a life of social combat. Thin, weasel-faced, sharp-eyed, he rejects pressure from his father Francois-Marie Arouet, a prominent Paris lawyer, to join his legal practice. He revels instead in Paris high society which accepts him for a titillating torrent of plays, pamphlets and verse with which he entertains it. To complete the family rift and burnish his salon standing, he abandons the Arouet name, which he rates commonplace, in favour of the grander-sounding Voltaire (a felicitous anagram of family name and his initials). Salon glory bites back. Mocking verses he composes in his early twenties on amorous foibles at the royal court land him in the Bastille dungeons for a harsh eleven-month stay. He emerges with satiric quill sharpened, only to be thrown back later into the Bastille after an acid public dispute with a nobleman who enjoys royal favour. This time he is freed after two weeks on condition he leave the country, which he does, finding hospitable refuge in London. Much impressed by the freedom of opinion he encounters in England, he vows after three years in exile to bring it back with him to Louis XV's France, a mission he achieves with cutting wit in his *Lettres Philosophiques*, a brazen tilt at royal power and Church dogma.

Scandal! Much as he tries to conceal his authorship, a recourse at which he is growing adept, his reward is banishment to the provinces, where he further whets his satire in the comfort of a high-born mistress's chateau and later following a three-year stay in Berlin at the invitation of Prussian monarch Frederick II, who is fascinated by his cussed views – at his own French hideaway in the village of Ferney across the Swiss border from Geneva, where he writes *Candide*.

Voltaire dies a tantalising eleven years before the French Revolution aged eighty-four, the lodestar of the Enlightenment unaware of the staggering changes his pen will bring.

***

W IS FOR

WATERLOO

The France Alphabet

A small place in Belgium. A most doleful place in the French soul. *Waterloo, Waterloo, that dismal plain...* Victor Hugo's lament captures French sentiment on Napoleon's last battle (June 1815). The most painstakingly analysed battle of all time arouses not lasting French fury with the damned English for having inflicted so memorable a defeat – one worse than Trafalgar – but rather a feeling of melancholy that Waterloo happens as it does, indeed that it should have happened at all.

Even in Napoleon's day his rush to engage in the battle of Waterloo in Europe's soggy lowlands – a saga of carnage that will take the lives of around a third of 350,000 French, British, German and Dutch troops involved – wins faint support in France.

One hundred days have passed since the lately deposed French emperor's escape from the Mediterranean islet of Elba to which Europe's victorious allied powers have benignly exiled him, confident they have disposed of him once and for all. They were wrong. Stouter now at forty-five, the escaping Napoleon reaches

France's Mediterranean shore and marches to Paris to reclaim his lost throne, encouraged on his way by cries of *Vive l'Empereur* and a rush to his colours of veterans of his disbanded Grande Armée. The acclaim scarcely reflects the mood of the nation at large, which is mainly one of relief that his empire's endless warring is over.

Napoleon, impetuous as ever, now decides to strike first against his European adversaries, aware that the allied powers aim to crush him once more for breaking his exile. He rapidly forms a new army around his core of Grande Armée veterans to attack twin allied forces occupying Belgium – the Duke of Wellington's Anglo-Dutch army camped at Waterloo just west of Brussels and Marshal Blücher's Prussian army camped not far to the east. His plan is to drive a wedge between them, hold them apart, then destroy them one after the other before they muster to invade France. To prepare the defeat first of Wellington he successfully deploys part of his new army to push Blücher's forces further east, out of the way and out of contention.

At Waterloo it rains hard prior to the attack on Wellington's army. The ground underfoot is mush. Still, on the day, Napoleon's troops are threatening to overwhelm Wellington's redcoats in wave after muddied wave of French army blue. The British and the Dutch are still holding fast but in imminent danger of being overrun when out of nowhere Blücher miraculously arrives late in the day for their relief (Napoleon has initially mistaken Blücher's forces for his own and ignored them). For Wellington the day is won. Napoleon, crushed but escaping capture, returns to France to abdicate anew.

French melancholy over Waterloo is akin to doleful British pride in the Light Brigade's hopeless charge in the Crimea. The sentiment persists that Frenchmen have never fought more bravely than at Waterloo and that only misunderstandings between Napoleon's generals are to blame for turning gallant victory into defeat. It is a sentiment wrapped in pathos. Worship France's greatest soldier or not, Waterloo truly is his swansong.

***

X IS FOR XXL

The France Alphabet

X IS FOR XXL

XXL is a size conspicuous for its absence in France. The French are a slim people, the least obese in all Europe. Search for XXL, even XL, in a quality French clothing store and you will leave empty-handed.

The absence of the outsize carries a certain mystery all the same. French women with their seemingly natural slenderness and knack of staying slender with age are used to serving as a role model for figure-conscious Western womenfolk. Paris is a woman's city. Svelte Marianne is France's national symbol. Yet the French, women as well as men, consume more wine than any other people on earth – some fifty litres a year per head on average, mainly red. Ostensibly they also eat as 'fatly' as anyone else, since butter, cheese, cream, potato chips and red meat are high on the national menu.

Thus the French paradox. While eschewing the weightwatcher's handbook, the French come out slim. High self-awareness about personal appearance helps. Culture most definitely helps. There is a lot in what French mothers pass on to their daughters. The real trick, however, is the *way* the French eat. They eat better. French restaurants don't pile plates high with food, they serve moderate portions, to be eaten slowly, savoured, digested at leisure, over table talk, wine and mineral water. The accent is on quality not quantity. Also on freshness and balance. The French eat some of everything, and more besides – frogs and horses at a pinch – but eat less overall. And while they feast on wine, they go easy on beer. They down only a third as much beer per head as Germans, half as much as Americans and the British, all of whom weigh-in considerably more obese.

But wait. The slenderness culture is at risk. The French, not least the working class, are not physiologically immune to putting on weight. When McDonald's is able to announce, as it has, fatter profits in France than anywhere else in Europe, a challenge looms for the national waistline. Breathe in, Marianne.

***

Y IS FOR YORE

France is a modern nation in the world forefront of fashion, science, technology and much else besides. Look elsewhere, though, for the French national identity. Look to the ups and downs of a past stretching back 2000 years. Look back over the days of yore – to France ever fighting a running battle with history to make herself whole and keep herself whole.

A potted calendar of yore:

52 BC – Vercingetorix, tribal chief of primitive Gauls, fights a losing battle on home turf against Julius Caesar, a defeat that brings Roman civilisation to the land of the Gauls in what will become central France.

496 – With the Roman Empire falling apart, Clovis, king of barbarian Franks from the north, drives south to conquer the Gauls, merging the two peoples under his Merovingian dynasty's rule and lending the realm a name: France.

732 – At Poitiers, Frankish ruler Charles Martel beats back a Moorish Arab invasion cutting deep into France. Saved from Moorish domination, France becomes a prominent Christian power.

800 – Charlemagne, Charles Martel's conquering grandson, is crowned emperor of a re-created Roman Empire which he splits into separate tranches – east, middle and west – for his three sons. In the French western slice regional lords pit themselves against the French crown.

987 – A northern regional lord Hugh Capet takes the throne to halt the disunited realm's disintegration, implanting a dynasty will rule for eight hundred years.

1066 – William, sovereign Duke of Normandy, invades England to mount the English throne, bringing a primitive folk from across the Channel into French history. An ill omen, this. William's English descendants assert sovereignty not only over Normandy (Battle of Agincourt, **1415**) but over much else of France besides.

1429 – Joan of Arc inspires resistance to English territorial dominance in France, ensuring the survival of the Capetian crown.

1598 – Religious wars pitting the Catholic Church against Protestant (Huguenot) reformers, source of half a century of domestic bloodshed, are halted by reform-minded Henri IV under his Edict of Nantes.

1661 – Louis XIV, the Sun King, begins a reign that makes France the strongest power in Europe. He consolidates France within her 'natural frontiers' extending French hegemony across the Rhine into Germany as well, but also revokes the Edict of Nantes.

1789 – The French Revolution. France becomes a republic.

1804 – Napoleon Bonaparte takes power on the back of glorious military exploits for revolutionary France, then crowns himself French Emperor, conquering far and wide across Europe before final defeat (**1815**) at Waterloo.

1870 – A triumphant Prussia invades France and lays lengthy siege to Paris to pave the way for German unification, annexing Alsace and industrial Lorraine in the process.

1914 – In alliance with Britain and the United States, France has her revenge on Germany in the Great War, taking back Alsace-Lorraine.

1940 – France is vanquished and occupied by Hitler's Germany, emerging scarred but whole at war's end, after which the French take the lead in uniting Europe.

You may calculate that on balance France's yore has more downs than ups, which may account for a related token of national identity – a native pessimism existing beside *art de vivre,* an appetite for self-flagellation, an incurable propensity to protest even when things are really not going badly at all. Should you be caught up in one of the mass demonstrations in which the French specialise, be patient. Yore will have its say.

***

Z IS FOR ZOLA

It must have perplexed and no doubt vexed Emile Zola (1840–1902) that his fame even during his lifetime is founded as much on a single indignant newspaper article as on a rich trove of novels on French society that places him in the pantheon of the widest-read French authors.

Zola, son of an Italian engineer who dies bankrupt when he is a child, is orphaned out by his impoverished French mother to his grandmother in Paris. He is a dud at school. He haunts the estaminets of bohemian Paris, falls in love with a teenage prostitute he aims to 'save' and befriends struggling Impressionist painters, Cezanne in particular, before finding an outlet in polemical journalism, turning a sharp republican pen against Emperor Napoleon III, the authoritarian monarch of his day.

Close to thirty and about to get married (to a different working-class girl), he plunges headlong into a prodigious literary project similar to Balzac's *Comédie Humaine* – a model he disputes, protesting that his literary lens is scientific as opposed to the social lorgnette of his famous contemporary, his elder by forty years. In twenty searching novels that take twenty-one years to complete – a novel per year being his publishing target – Zola paints a vast canvas of 'the human folly and shame' of life in Napoleon III's France seen through members of a single family, the Rougon-Macquarts. As glue for the series he uses hereditary traits that shape family members' lives in the adulterous city (*Thérèse Raquin*), in the working class (*L'Assommoir*), in the coal mines (*Germinal*), the taverns, the shops, the railways, banking and the army. His harsh, often coarse style – attacked as needlessly base by eminent fellow authors envious of his success – indeed differs from Balzac's more compassionate pen.

No sooner has Zola breasted the finishing tape of this literary marathon than his restless moral juices are stirred by a huge public scandal that drives France to the brink of social civil war. The *Affaire Dreyfus* – the case of an upright French army captain

Z IS FOR ZOLA

cashiered from the army on false evidence and jailed for treason essentially because he is a Jew – is the stuff of bitter hostility between French liberals and conservative nationalists into which Zola lobs an incendiary cannon shell. In a Paris newspaper diatribe headlined *J'Accuse!* he charges the French state itself as well as the army brass with wilful antisemitism. For his 'slanderous' pains Zola too is sentenced to jail, which he evades by finding exile for a year in London at the cost of forfeiting his property in Paris.

Not long after returning from exile, his pen having finally secured the release of Dreyfus and seen him restored to officer rank, Zola, henceforth feted by liberals as France's moral conscience, dies a strange death at sixty-two, asphyxiated in his Paris bed by fumes from the fire in his bedroom fireplace. Assassination theories abound. Unforgiving nationalists snicker. They alone contest Zola's immense contribution to French letters.